Military Aircraft Library
Bombers

Military Aircraft Library
Bombers

DR. DAVID BAKER

Rourke Enterprises, Inc.
Vero Beach, FL 32964

BOMBERS

The Rockwell International B-1 bomber will be the mainstay of Strategic Air Command throughout the rest of this century as a weapons platform for cruise missiles and free-falling nuclear bombs, in addition to carrying out the duties of a low-level strike plane penetrating deep into enemy air space.

Library of Congress Cataloging-in-Publication Data

Baker, David, 1944-
  Bombers.

  (Military aircraft library)
  Includes index.
  Summary: Describes the design of various types of bombers, their uses in combat, and their role in the future.
  1. Bombers—United States—Juvenile literature.
[1. Bombers. 2. Airplanes, Military] I. Title.
II. Series: Baker, David, 1944-   . Military planes.
UG1242.B6B35 1987   358.4'2'0973   87-3357
ISBN 0-86592-355-8

CONTENTS

The Bomber's Role

Intercontinental Ballistic Missiles (ICBMs) are one of three different types of strategic weapon in the "triad" deterrent force. Here, a Minuteman ICBM is seen getting away from its silo in Vandenberg, California, on a test flight.

ICBMs are vulnerable because they are housed in silos covered with a large concrete door that could be shattered under a direct hit from an incoming nuclear weapon.

For a very long time, the bomber's role consisted of three objectives: to support land battles by destroying the enemy's supplies and his ability to keep fighting; to destroy the enemy's industrial facilities and prevent him replacing lost planes, tanks and guns; and to attack the enemy's cities in an attempt to break the public will to resist. Since the 1960s, the last objective has largely disappeared. Long-range missiles have replaced the bomber in that role. The bomber's job today is more concerned with curtailing the enemy's ability to keep fighting. The bomber must also try to knock out any enemy's strategic weapons before they can be launched.

Strategic weapons are those built to threaten countries with attack on their industries or military bases. Intercontinental ballistic missiles, (ICBMs) are strategic, because they can be launched against any country on earth. Tactical weapons are those used against armies on a battlefield or against air and naval forces massing for a specific attack. Today bombers

are used for both tactical and strategic jobs. They still carry out the first two primary objectives, to hit the enemy's supply lines and to destroy his industrial facilities. Their third objective has changed, however. It is now, to provide insurance against a sudden attack on United States missile sites.

The United States maintains a "triad" of strategic defense weapons: intercontinental ballistic missiles, submarine-launched ballistic missiles (SLBMs), and manned bombers. Should an enemy country make a major breakthrough in attacking any one of these three categories of weapon, two others remain to deter aggression. Consequently, the enemy would still have to suffer retaliation from one or both of the remaining systems. The bomber force, like ICBMs and SLBMs, is equipped to deliver such a mighty punch that no country would openly provoke attack. In that way, the deterrent is not only maintained, but it is insured as well.

To accomplish all three objectives, air force

The second leg of the strategic triad is carried in submarines and comprises long range missiles like ICBMs which are fired from beneath the sea. In this view of a submarine being assembled its twenty-four firing tubes are easily visible.

bombers are operated in two specific ways. In one kind of mission, the manned plane has to penetrate hostile airspace and fly deep inside enemy territory. It must find and destroy hidden targets in remote regions. It must also get back out again, either returning to base or, more likely, flying on to a friendly country where it can land. The bomber's other mission requirement is to fly close to the airspace of an enemy country and launch a *stand-off* weapon. This weapon will propel itself into enemy airspace and be guided to the target.

Sometimes the bomber is not expected to attack at all. If tension between countries increases to the point where war might break out, bombers are expected to pose a warning. They do this by presenting an unstoppable threat, demonstrating to the potential aggressor that he would gain nothing by attack. In fact, he would only bring upon himself an unacceptable retaliation. This is why the United States Defense Department wants to maintain a deterrent that relies on people rather than computers. Once fired, big missile systems like ICBMs and SLBMs

The third leg of the United States strategic deterrent is carried in the manned bomber force, represented here by a B-1.

In the last fifty years, bombers have grown from being an extension of land warfare to a fully independent weapon system capable of wreaking great destruction over wide areas.

cannot be turned back. Of all strategic weapons, only the manned bomber can be ordered to return without releasing its bombs.

Besides carrying out the duties they were designed for, bombers often handle other jobs as well. Some bombers have been equipped to lay mines down to stop enemy ships passing through narrow waterways. Sea mines usually weigh less than a load of bombs, so many can be carried and released into the water. Other duties include reconnaissance. In the 1940s and 1950s, this was a very important job. Only the bombers had the range and the speed to carry out mapping tasks with precision. These maps were necessary for accurate targeting in wartime. Since then, satellites have replaced reconnaissance versions of manned bombers, and special high speed planes have been built for this purpose.

Designing a Bomber

Bombers have existed almost as long as airplanes. Twelve years after the first powered flight in 1903, German bombers were raiding London, England. By the end of the First World War (1914-18), all the fighting powers were involved in attacking targets by dropping bombs on enemy positions. By the time of the Second World War (1939-45), bombers were being designed to fly several hundred miles. When WW II ended, the United States had put together a force of large planes capable of carrying huge bomb loads over several thousand miles. It was the beginning of a truly strategic bombing capability unlike anything seen before.

The plane that made it possible was the Boeing B-29 Superfortress. With a cruising speed of 290 MPH, this plane could lift a 20,000-pound bomb load and had a maximum range of more than 3,200 miles. It was built in large numbers and played a major role in the war against Japan. Operating from islands in the Pacific Ocean, B-29s were sent to bomb Japanese cities

Although it arrived late during the Second World War, the Boeing B-29 Superfortress was the world's first truly strategic bomber, capable of carrying not only high explosives but the first atomic bombs.

The explosive force of a small atomic bomb like that used on Hiroshima and Nagasaki, Japan, in 1945, is equal to the full bomb load of more than five hundred B-29s. This is mainstreet, Nagasaki, about a quarter mile from the center of the atom blast.

and industrial facilities. On some raids, more than 500 bombers took part, collectively dropping more than 2,000 tons of bombs on a single mission. The B-29 was used to drop atomic bombs on Hiroshima and Nagasaki in 1945. Each bomb had an explosive force equal to 20,000 tons of ordinary bombs.

Suddenly, because of the atomic bomb, the long-range bomber became a weapon of awesome power. Even before the war ended,

work was well under way on a replacement for the B-29. It was to be powered by six jet engines and had swept-back wings. With a speed of 560 MPH, it had a slightly greater range than the B-29 but could carry more than 22,000 pounds. This plane, known as the B-47 Stratojet, made its first flight in December, 1947. Before it became fully operational, however, the air force took possession of a truly incredible plane called the B-36 Peacemaker.

Built by Convair (now General Dynamics) as the first intercontinental range bomber, the B-36 Peacemaker was the last of the old piston engined strategic deterrents.

Built by Convair, the B-36 was designed to provide a means by which the United States could bomb Nazi Germany if England was invaded and U.S. military forces were unable to use bases in England to liberate the European continent. It was a colossal plane with a fuselage 162 feet long, a wing that spanned 230 feet, and a tail that stood nearly 47 feet above the ground. The Peacemaker carried a maximum bomb load of 84,000 pounds, equal to more than four B-29s, and could attack targets more than 8,000 miles from base. It had six big pusher engines, with the propellers at the back, and had a crew of almost 30.

Within two years from the time the B-36 entered service, a new version was built. From then on, all B-36s had, in addition to the six piston engines, four jet engines in twin pods near the wing tips. This was unofficially referred to as a "six turning, four burning" engine layout. The jets helped the plane get off the ground and were then shut down. During long distance flight, some of the propeller engines were shut down also.

The enormous bomb load of the B-36 was carried in two large bays. A special tunnel connected the pressure compartment at the front with one at the rear where the off-duty crew slept and had their meals. Crew members moving from one to the other would pull themselves along the tunnel on a little trolley. On a full range mission, a B-36 could be airborne up to 42

At first, the B-36 had six pusher engines driving propellers, but later versions like this shown here added four jet engines in two outboard pods.

hours. They frequently were. Hot meals were prepared in the galley, and the two flight crew teams took turns at the controls. The B-36 could fly at a height of more than 45,000 feet and spent most of its long-duration missions close to this altitude.

The B-36 joined the U.S. Air Force in 1948, and 385 were built before it was retired in 1958. By this time the B-47 Stratojet was the mainstay of Strategic Air Command, or SAC. Formed in 1946, SAC was responsible for the strategic deterrent. It built up its forces until, by 1959, SAC had 3,200 planes of which nearly 1,400 were the Stratojets. Its motto, "Peace Is Our Profession," stands on the headquarters gate at Offutt Air Force Base, Nebraska. The motto is a fitting reminder of SAC's responsibility.

One development that never materialized was this plan to have a B-36 carry its own fighter escort on a carriage beneath the plane's belly.

The B-52

Sleek, and much smaller than the B-36 in service, this five-engined Boeing B-47 brought a new look to bomber design. Note the long range fuel tanks between the engine pods.

Following hard on the heels of the B-47, the most durable and lasting bomber design of the post-war period was the B-52, seen in this cutaway. It had a crew of six, and wheels that folded up inside the main body of plane between the bomb bays, with eight engines in four pods and an option for long range fuel tanks fitted under each wing tip.

Before the end of the Second World War in 1945, the United States looked beyond the day when peace would return and thought about weapons it would need to prevent such a war from ever happening again. Many people thought the war had been caused by a lack of readiness to deter aggression. The dictators in Europe and Japan that caused the war thought they could win a quick battle and overwhelm neighboring countries. They could not, and the United States had to send several million men and thousands of weapons to help overpower the dictators.

What the United States wanted for its peacetime air force was a weapon so powerful that no one would dare start a war in the future. Serious work began in 1946 to design a heavy bomber capable of carrying atomic weapons 6,000 miles at 400 MPH. At this time the Boeing Airplane Company was building the B-47 Strato-

jet. This was a medium bomber first designed in 1943 at the request of the air force, who wanted a jet-powered reconnaissance plane capable of being converted into a bomber. Now the air force wanted a heavy bomber to act as a strategic deterrent.

Boeing had done much work on high-performance, long-range, heavy bombers. It designed and built the B-17 Fortress which was used in great numbers to bomb enemy targets. It also built the B-29 Superfortress, which did so much to end the war in the Pacific by destroying Japan's ability to make weapons. With new ideas about high-speed plane design emerging as a result of great strides in aviation, the heavy bomber was a logical step forward for this company. Boeing prepared several different designs, but many advances in knowledge were taking place and the requirements kept changing. Finally in 1950 they came up with the plane the

With a design dating back to the early 1950s the B-52's flight deck relies heavily on dials despite the update incorporating two computer screen displays. Notice the old fashioned yoke control columns and the eight throttle levers, white knobs on levers in foreground.

The B-52 was considerably faster than any of its predecessors and had a range with full war load that could carry it unrefuelled a quarter way round the world.

air force wanted. It was to be called the B-52 Stratofortress.

In the five years since it was first discussed, the B-52 had gone from a 400-MPH, propeller-driven plane to a 650-MPH, eight-engine jet. With swept wings and a huge tail so tall it had to fold down to get in the hangar, the big bomber appeared in November, 1951. The first flight came five months later followed by several changes which altered the shape of the cockpit. Instead of a tandem arrangement, the two pilots sitting one behind the other, production planes would place them side by side. Throughout the life of the B-52, seven major versions would be introduced as developments improved performance. These would make a few visual differences to the familiar shape. Most identifiable features were retained throughout the program.

The B-52 has a wing span of 185 feet and a length of 160 feet. To put this in perspective, if two B-52s were placed wing tip to wing tip lengthwise on a football field, a wing tip of each airplane would extend 35 feet beyond the goal line. The bodies of the two planes would extend the full width of the field. The B-52 usually carries a crew of six, with two seated behind and below the pilots and two farther back. It carries a set of four machine guns, or a single cannon, in the tail for defense against attacking planes.

Most of the time it relies on electronic jammers to confuse enemy radar.

With a total weight of more than 244 tons, each B-52 contains well over one half million rivets, 18,000 pieces of wire measuring 57 miles in length, and generates enough electricity to run 70 average homes. The plane stands on four *bogies*, each with two wheels, arranged in pairs to the left and right of the fuselage. Wing tip mounted wheels keep the wings balanced for takeoff and landing.

The B-52 entered service with the air force Strategic Air Command in June, 1955. Peak strength was reached in 1962 when SAC had 639 planes in service. In all, 744 B-52s were built in two huge production facilities, one at Wichita, Kansas, and the other at Seattle, Washington. The plane saw extensive service in Vietnam and was modified to increase its 27,000-pound bomb load to a capacity of 70,000 pounds. Today, SAC has about 240 B-52s in service.

The last version of this giant bomber, the B-52H, has many improvements over its predecessors and will probably be the mainstay of Strategic Air Command well into the 1990s. Note the larger turbofan engines and a shorter tail.

Diverse Roles

The enormous success of bomber programs like the B-52 posed a seemingly unchallenged threat to ground forces in hostile territory. Consequently, very considerable efforts have been made to stop the bomber getting through. More than ever, it needs special defenses to help protect it and survive devastating fire power from the ground.

Big bombers like the B-52 Stratofortress were designed to carry atomic weapons across great distances to targets many thousands of miles away. The B-52 was a modern replacement for the huge, lumbering, B-36 Peacemaker. Although capable of carrying more than 80,000 pounds of bombs, it was slow and vulnerable. This was mainly because it did not have the speed to move quickly to its target or the sophisticated electronics necessary to escape detection. Planes like the B-52 were built to take advantage of technical developments that gave the bomber an even chance in hostile airspace. It is a concept called survivability.

When the B-52 appeared, it changed the way air force planners envisioned the bomber's role. Before it entered service, Strategic Air Command operated planes capable of carrying high-explosive bombs. They had been adapted to carry atomic weapons in the late 1940s. The

B-52, however, was the first heavy bomber to be designed from the outset for flying high and fast with a nuclear warload. When the United States successfully detonated its first *hydrogen bomb* in 1952, it had a very powerful weapon unlike anything used before.

When atomic weapons were developed and used against Japan in 1945, each bomb had ten times the explosive power of a massed air raid of 500 B-29s dropping high explosive bombs. The hydrogen bomb, or thermonuclear weapon, had potentially the explosive force of between 500 and 1,000 atom bombs. Each B-52 could carry several small hydrogen bombs or one big one. The first hydrogen bombs were big and weighed a lot. Breakthroughs in weapon technology considerably reduced the size of thermonuclear weapons in the 1950s. More bombs could be carried or, because the load was lighter, fewer bombs over greater distances.

To make the B-52 look less visible on radar screens and to provide confusion for anti-aircraft defenses, some bombers carried this Quail decoy which had the radar "signature" of a full size B-52 making many targets to attack instead of one.

Nuclear weapons are not used like high-explosive bombs, because they have a much more devastating effect on people and the environment. A strict military rule, common to land, sea, and air conflict, is never to use more force than necessary to achieve an objective. To do so would reduce the number of weapons left over to deter further attack. It could also provoke an enemy to reckless behavior. Only in the event that the very existence of the United States was threatened by awesome and overwhelming forces would any consideration ever be given to the use of nuclear weapons. This policy means that unless the bombers can also use conventional bombs, they are useless except as a passive deterrent.

To give the nuclear armed B-52 force a con-ventional role, modifications were made to enable one version, the B-52D, to carry a very large load of high explosives. This plane was used mainly in Vietnam, where it supported other B-52 planes capable only of carrying the basic 27,000-pound warload. Before that, however, the bomber was given the job of carrying large powered missiles that could fly independently to their targets. One, called Skybolt, was cancelled before it entered service, while the other, Hound Dog, remained with SAC between 1959 and 1978. Hound Dog could fly a distance of 500 miles and each B-52 carried a single missile under each wing.

The B-52 has been used extensively for many different research tasks. As a heavyweight, it is useful for carrying into the air planes that can-

To give the bomber added survivability, the powered Hound Dog stand-off missile was developed so that bombers could release them outside enemy air space. Hound Dog would then propel itself to the target.

not get off the ground under their own power. These range from the X-15 rocket-powered research plane to strange unpowered test planes like miniature versions of the NASA shuttle. The X-15 had a powerful rocket engine for speeds up to *Mach* 6 (six times the speed of sound) but had to be carried up under the wing of a B-52 before beginning its independent flight. To try ways of controlling a spacecraft returning from orbit, the B-52 was used to lift into the air planes called *Lifting Bodies*. With a blended wing and body, these planes helped provide the information engineers wanted to design the shuttle.

This version, the B-52D, was modified due to experience in Vietnam which demonstrated a need for an "iron-bomber". This version could carry about 80,000 pounds of bombs.

Because of their enormous size, bombers like the B-52 have been used for many other duties, including the launch in midair of a rocket propelled X-15 research plane.

The Bomber's Warload

Known as the Short Range Attack Missile, this weapon can be carried by the FB-111A, the B-52 and the B-1. It is used against targets up to one hundred miles away.

This rotary launcher carries SRAM missiles in the weapon bay of a bomber, from there they are released one at a time to fly separately to their respective targets.

Although much slower than the SRAM, cruise missiles fly at 535 mph but travel great distances. This version can fly a winding and circuitous, preprogramed route, a total distance of about 1,700 miles with a nuclear warhead.

With its existing range of B-52 bombers, the U.S. Air Force has one of the most powerful deterrents in the world. Each is capable of carrying 70,000 pounds of conventional or nuclear bombs. Since 1986, the Rockwell B-1B has been coming into service, and it can carry a warload weighing 125,000 pounds with a mix of different weapons. Each plane has the strike power of all the bombs, rockets, and shells ever used in war.

Today, bombers generally use one of two techniques to hit the enemy. The first uses either conventional (high-explosive) or nuclear weapons and is called free-fall bombing, where the plane has to fly directly over the target and release its load. The second is called stand-off bombing, where the plane drops a missile that uses a rocket engine or jet motor to propel the warhead several hundred miles to its target. In the first method, the bomber is exposed to enemy air defenses, which are usually clustered round the target under attack. In the second method, the bomber can release its weapon far away and escape the heavy defenses.

Free-fall bombing has the advantage that only one system can fail: the bomber. If the bomber gets through, all the bombs will hit their targets. If a bomber releases, for instance, 24 rocket-propelled stand-off weapons, not all of them will get through the enemy defenses. Many could be shot down. Alternatively, as some people point out, sending 24 rocket-powered missiles through enemy air space makes it more likely that the majority will get through. Military experts who oppose free-fall bombing say that only one target in the sky, the bomber itself, has to be hit for none of the bombs to reach their intended destinations.

With many technical developments producing more accurate anti-aircraft defenses each year, the U.S. Air Force prefers to use bombers in a stand-off mode. Accordingly, there are two major weapon types that U.S. bombers carry for different jobs. One is called the Short Range Attack Missile, or *SRAM*. Attacking ground targets between 37 miles and 100 miles away, the SRAM is boosted by a powerful rocket motor to three times the speed of sound, about 1,980 MPH. SRAM is only 14 feet long but carries a powerful nuclear punch to destroy enemy sites. In one application, it can be used to help clear a path for the bombers to get through and drop free-fall bombs, but the SRAM is usually carried as part of a warload mix.

In some missions it might be used to clear the path for another form of stand-off weapon, the cruise missile. Cruise missiles have been pro-

Cruise missiles carried on external mountings on B-52 planes are usually carried in "six-pack" pylons, one under each wing.

duced in large numbers for use from aircraft, surface ships, submarines, and from ground launchers. The Air Launched Cruise Missile, *ALCM*, is 20.75 feet long but much slower than the rocket-propelled SRAM. With a tiny *turbofan* engine it literally "cruises" to its target at around 535 MPH, little more than one-quarter the speed of SRAM. Yet it can fly a distance of up to 1,730 miles, weaving a twisting and winding path, hugging the ground as it goes. Because it flies so low, it has a better chance of evading enemy radar.

The ALCM carries a similar warhead to the SRAM and is extremely accurate, being able to hit targets to within 25 feet at maximum range. It does this by storing computer maps of its route and comparing the course it should be taking with radar scans of the approaching terrain. It takes scans every so often and corrects the course to a precise track, making more frequent scans as it nears its pre-determined target. In this way, continually updating and correcting for errors, the ALCM achieves an accuracy over

great distances that free-falling bombs would be unable to achieve.

For most long-range bombing missions in a major war, the bomber would never even need to enter hostile air space. Only the automated and fully programmed cruise missiles would fly through the intense heat of enemy anti-aircraft fire. Some scientists are working on cruise weapons capable of having their flight paths changed after being dropped from bombers. In this way, satellites in space can watch for patrolling enemy fighters and order the low-flying missiles to change course and stay out of their way, discreetly creeping up on their targets.

With a length of less than 21 feet, the air launched cruise missile stows its wings and tail until released for flight. The small engine seen here to the left is a developed version of the motor used to power agricultural crop spraying planes.

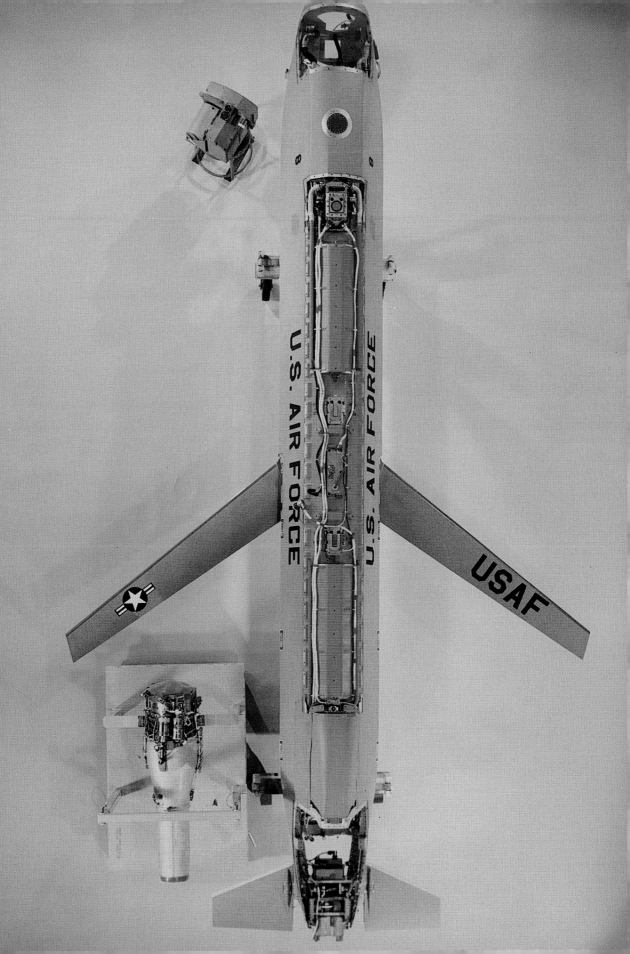

Threats to the Bomber

One of the threats to the long range, high-speed bomber, developed in direct response to planes built in the United States, is this Russian Mig-25 Foxbat capable of Mach 3.

The devastating effect of heavy bombing during the Second World War resulted in many countries putting major efforts into defense against air attack. Not least was the Soviet Union, which built up during the 1950s a formidable defense against planes trying to enter Russian airspace. The United States is part of *NATO*, the North Atlantic Treaty Organization, which includes Canada, Britain, and several European countries. Under this agreement, all NATO countries are pledged to go to the aid of any one country that receives unprovoked attack. Only the United States has the long-range bomber force to penetrate deep inside Soviet airspace.

Fighters are primarily designed to attack strike planes flying at low altitude. They can also go after the bombers, including those that are several hundred miles away from the border. With stand-off weapons, even the distant bombers lurking far over the horizon are a

Another, more recent threat is the Mig-29 Fulcrum seen here with a full load of anti-aircraft missiles.

threat because they release weapons that fly independently to their assigned targets. It is most effective to attack the bomber before it releases these weapons. This may be very difficult, because the bomber might be very low and hard to find. Radar waves usually travel in straight lines. If the bomber is down over the horizon, air-defense radar antenna from land-based sites in enemy territory will not locate the bomber. This means the fighters have to search on their own. To hunt for the bomber, they might have to leave the protection of their own airspace.

One Soviet fighter plane was designed and built to combat the United States bomber force. Back in the late 1950s, when the air force talked about having a supersonic bomber, the Russian Mig airplane company came up with an interceptor capable of reaching more than three times the speed of sound. The U.S. Air Force never did get the truly supersonic bomber the Russians feared, but the Mig made its first flight in 1964. At the time, it was the fastest plane around. Officially called Mig-25, it was known as the Foxbat. The plane had two very powerful Turmanskii turbojets, each with a maximum thrust of more than 24,000 MPH above 36,000 feet. Like all planes, the Foxbat becomes slower in lower altitudes and can achieve only 650 MPH at sea level.

Identified in particular as a threat to penetrating bombers like the B-52, which cannot easily fly at very low altitude, is this Russian built Mig-31 Foxhound, also carrying air-to-air missiles.

Soviet Tu-16/BADGER Combat Radius From Cam Ranh Airfield

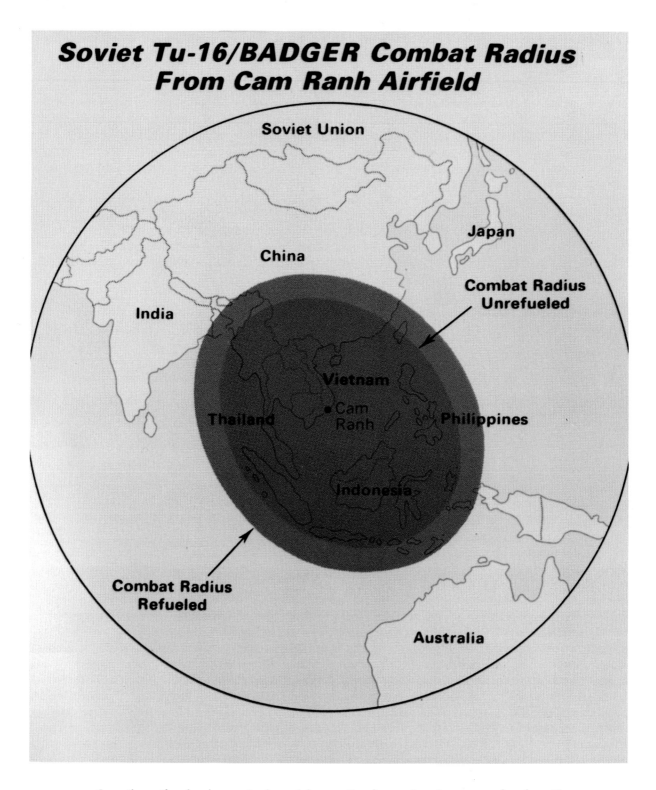

Sometimes the development of special operating bases gives long range bombers the capability of hitting targets they would not otherwise be able to reach; this diagram shows the combat radius of a Soviet TU-16 bomber force operating from the Vietnamese base at Cam Rahn Bay.

There are about 470 Foxbat interceptors in the Soviet air force, although 170 are used for reconnaissance. These 170 planes are equipped with cameras and other special sensors. The Mig-25 is not much good in combat. Its sheer power gives it the ability to go after high-speed targets far away from defense sites on the Soviet homeland. It is, however, little more than a missile launcher, and when these weapons are gone it is vulnerable to attack. The real air threat to the bomber probably comes from the Mig-31 Foxhound. Developed from the Foxbat, the plane has a top speed of 1,500 MPH and is much more deadly. It has radar that can "see" targets at very low altitude, and missiles that can attack speeding planes only 200 feet above the ground.

By far the most awesome threat to bombers entering Soviet airspace is the large number of surface-to-air missiles, called *SAMs*, which the Russians have built up over the last thirty years. They have more than 9,000 SAM launchers at 1,300 sites, and each can fire many missiles.

The most severe threat to the manned penetrating bomber is the surface-to-air missile, represented here by this SA-5 weapon built and deployed by the Soviet Union.

Some of these launchers are mobile, while others are at fixed bases. With sensitive radar equipment, they cover almost every approach to Soviet territory. For many years the SAM sites have been seen as a major obstacle to penetrating bombers. This is one reason so much attention has been given to the development of stand-off weapons. Should the need arise, they can be dropped from bombers far outside Russian airspace. Nevertheless, some missions might need bombers to penetrate the areas protected by SAMs. The United States is developing a bomber for such a purpose, having come to believe that the SAM sites are indeed a real threat.

Supersonic Bombers

The fastest bomber yet brought into operational use was the Convair, now General Dynamics, B-58 Hustler. It remained with Strategic Air Command for the duration of the 1960s.

In the late 1940s, the air force wanted a supersonic bomber to fly at very great heights. Missiles were expected to eventually become a major threat to high-flying planes, but the fighter was still the dominant threat. Military planners reasoned that a bomber that flew faster and higher than the fighters could avoid being shot down and would survive when penetrating hostile air space.

By 1952, the Convair airplane manufacturer had been given a contract for developing the design of a supersonic bomber. It is important to remember that at this time the first production jet fighter to achieve Mach 1 in level flight had not yet flown. Technology had to move fast to keep up with what the air force wanted.

In 1953, Convair discovered an important detail about supersonic plane design. Called *area-rule*, this aerodynamic design provides a smooth flow of air around the region where the wing joins the body of the plane. The concept was discovered when another Convair plane, the

F-102 fighter, designed to fly at Mach 1.3, refused to go through the speed of sound. Engineers found that by shaping the body like a coke bottle, it would slip easily through Mach 1! This discovery was made just in time to give the supersonic bomber a Coke-bottle fuselage.

The Convair B-58 appeared in 1956, making its first flight on November 11. It was small for the role it had been designed to accomplish. The plane had a length of 97 feet and a span across its delta-shaped wing of less than 57 feet. The Hustler, as it was called, had an enormous pod underneath capable of carrying cameras, weapons, or fuel. The Hustler needed lots of fuel. Even with tanks in the wings, the fuselage and the pod, the plane had a range of only 5,125 miles. That gave it a combat radius of less than 2,600 miles. It had to be refueled in the air by a tanker plane to achieve the range the air force needed.

The B-58 had a bomb load of about 19,000 pounds and could carry other weapons in addi-

The B-58 carried three crew members, one behind the other, but did not have the weight capability to deliver large bomb loads over great distances.

tion to nuclear bombs. It cost a lot to run and was too short on performance to be a useful part of Strategic Air Command. The Hustler entered service during 1960, and ten years later it was withdrawn. Nevertheless, it was the first of a completely new generation, the world's first moderately successful supersonic bomber. With a speed of Mach 2, about 1,322 MPH, it was very useful as a reconnaissance plane, and some

With a "swing wing" the Air Force F-111 was an ideal choice for developing a low altitude supersonic bomber capable of penetrating deep into enemy territory unseen by radar units.

Known as the FB-111A, and seen here with its bomb bay open revealing a SRAM on the left, this converted fighter-bomber has been in service with SAC since 1970.

Low-flying intruders like the FB-111A would come under threat from mobile anti-aircraft gun systems like this Soviet ZSU-X.

were operated in this role.

When the B-58 slipped out of service during 1970, a new supersonic bomber entered service. This plane was the FB-111, built by General Dynamics, the company that took over Convair. The FB-111 began life as a fighter built for both air force and navy use. The navy dropped out when the plane got too heavy to operate from aircraft carriers, leaving the air force with the basis for a rugged, all-weather strike plane. It had the structural strength to carry heavy loads and a capacity for long-duration flights.

The bomber version had a maximum weight of more than 114,000 pounds and could lift a warload of 37,500 pounds. Compared with the B-58, which weighed 163,000 pounds and carried a 19,000-pound warload, the FB-111 had a more efficient design. It was also simpler to operate and carried two crew members in a comfortable cockpit where both men sat side by side. The B-58 carried three crew members, one behind the other in sealed compartments. The FB-111 did not have great range, managing little more than a 2,000 mile distance with full weapons load. However, it was able to penetrate enemy airspace very low down and avoid detection by radar until the very last minute. About 55 FB-111s remain in service.

Long before the last B-58 was retired, the development of surface-to-air missiles made it almost impossible for manned bombers to survive at high speed and high altitude. The only way bombers would have any chance of getting through was to fly very low, close to the ground. That way they could avoid detection by radar and have a better chance of survival.

The Rockwell B-1B

The Strategic Air Command exists to help deter aggression that could lead to war, as its motto indicates. Nevertheless, it stands guard on the strategic interests of the United States and must be ready to go to war if necessary. To do that effectively, it must have the proper equipment. Accordingly, SAC has begun to operate a long-range bomber capable of supersonic speed at high altitude. Called the B-1B, it has been waiting a long time for this plane.

Back in the 1950s when the Boeing B-52 was coming into service, the air force asked plane makers to design a long-range bomber capable of cruising up to enemy territory at subsonic speed. Inside enemy airspace it would accelerate to supersonic speed and stay at that speed until it was safely outside again. There were big problems for designers at that time. Nobody knew how to achieve such speeds with a large plane. North American Aviation, now a part of the Rockwell Corporation, came up with a revolutionary answer.

They made a plane that could not only go supersonic in enemy airspace, but one that would immediately accelerate after takeoff to three times the speed of sound and stay at that astonishing speed all the way out and back. It could do this because, like a surfboard on the crest of a wave, it rode on the top of energy built up underneath the huge wing and body of the plane. This concept, known as *compression-lift*, made the plane much more efficient, cut down the fuel it needed, and gave it both speed and range.

The plane, called the B-70 Valkyrie, flew for the first time in 1964. By this time, ironically, plans to deploy it had been cancelled because top military officials believed high-flying

Built by Rockwell International, the B-1 is the latest penetrating bomber to enter service with Strategic Air Command, seen here against the spectacular backdrop of the Rockies.

High-flying bombers can no longer survive in enemy air space and the B-1 uses swing-wings to give it a better ride close to the ground. In this view it has its wings swept back for high-speed flights.

For low-altitude flight just below the speed of sound, the B-1 carries special radar scanners to "read" the terrain ahead and control the aircraft's movements to avoid obstacles while small control surfaces either side of the nose help to damp out what would otherwise be a rough, boneshaking ride for the crew.

bombers would not survive enemy missile fire. Anti-aircraft missiles had been developed to such a high degree that by the time the B-70 flew, it was already out of date. Now, the air force wanted a bomber that could fly very close to the ground. Outright speed was no longer as important as the ability to sneak into enemy airspace undetected. The B-70 could not fly close to the ground, so it was used until 1969 on high-speed flight research up to its top speed of more than 2,000 MPH.

The air force conducted many design studies to find the right kind of plane for low-level penetration of enemy airspace. By 1968 the specification had been settled and less than two years later Rockwell received a contract to build

Compared with the aging B-52, the B-1B has a modern, computerized, flight control system with controls like those found in a fighter. Note the advance strip recorders and computer screens for the complex radio, guidance and navigation systems.

what was now called the B-1 bomber. The plane had a *variable-geometry* wing, which swept back for high-speed flight and extended forward for low level penetration at subsonic speed. The B-1 could carry about twice the load of a B-52 at almost three times the speed. It promised to give SAC flexibility to fly conventional bombing missions or long-range nuclear strike missions.

Four B-1A planes were built, and a comprehensive test program got under way. The first flight took place in December, 1974, and the air force planned to buy 240 bombers of this type to replace aging B-52s. Less than three years later, President Jimmy Carter cancelled the plane and told the air force to make do with its remaining B-52s. He did allow testing to continue, but even this ended in 1981. During that year, President Reagan examined again the needs of SAC in improving its bomber force. The B-52 was a 30-year-old design, and the joke went around that many of its pilots were younger than the planes they flew! President Reagan restarted the program that had been abandoned, renaming the plane the B-1B, and the first modified plane flew in 1984.

The B-1B is a different plane from the B-1A. Gone is its high (Mach 2.2) speed for a heavier design capable of carrying 125,000 pounds of bombs and missiles. The B-1B can reach a top speed of Mach 1.4, but it is most useful low down, close to the ground, at just below the speed of sound. It has a range of 6,500 miles and entered service with the air force in 1986. SAC plans to operate a fleet of 100 B-1Bs.

Flanked by the B-52 (right) and the supersonic FB-111A (left), the B-1 is expected to remain in service for the rest of this century, eventually becoming a carrier for stand-off weapons when advances in air defense systems make it vulnerable to attack.

Typical Bombing Missions

The strategic bomber has many roles to play, from dropping conventional bombs to conducting a nuclear strike. The B-1B has awesome hitting power for both roles and many between. The two huge weapons bays inside the fuselage can be used to house a variety of bombs, stand-off weapons, and supplementary fuel tanks. In addition, special mountings on the outside allow for many more bombs.

As a conventional bomber dropping high-explosive bombs, the plane can carry 84 500-pound bombs internally and an additional 14 externally. The 98 bombs total 49,000 pounds. Or instead, it can carry 38 2,000-pound bombs, 24 inside and 14 outside. A conventional mission might begin with takeoff from a base in the United States. The plane might have to refuel from an airborne tanker, or it might be capable of flying all the way out and back on its internal fuel.

The B-1B would fly high at more than Mach 1 most of the way, descend as it approached enemy territory, and fly very low just below the speed of sound to avoid detection as long as possible. The plane has a special radar that looks down at the ground and automatically adjusts the controls to prevent it hitting obstacles like hills, trees, or buildings. From low altitude the bomber would release its load of bombs and make a dash for safety. It might fly straight back to the United States without refueling or rendezvous with a tanker plane to top up its tanks.

To give the B-52 added survivability most missions it would fly would keep it far from enemy air space. Equipped with cruise missiles on underwing pylons, the bomber would launch large numbers of these standoff weapons, each one of which would fly separately to its preprogramed target.

For a mission to launch cruise missiles, the bomber will probably not penetrate enemy airspace. Instead, it will operate in the stand-off role, releasing weapons close to but not over hostile territory. The B-1B carries up to 8 cruise missiles internally and 14 more on exterior pylons. Or it can carry a full load of SRAM (Short Range Attack Missiles) with 24 inside and 14 outside the plane's weapons bays. Because the SRAM is designed for destroying surface-to-air missile complexes, clearing the threat away before the bomber reaches it, a combination of SRAM and cruise missiles would be a more normal load for the B-lB.

Even long range bombers like the B-52 and the B-1 are sometimes unable to reach their targets without refueling on the way out and would not get back to base without refueling on the way home, as demonstrated here by this KC-135 tanker about to link up with a B-52.

The long range cruise missile gives added survivability to the bomber force while providing a large number of separate and independent targets for air defenses to attack.

In this configuration, a B-52 is equipped with eight SRAMs on two inboard pylons to supplement a load of internally mounted nuclear gravity bombs.

One of the more complex and daring missions would be a strike with free-falling nuclear bombs. Here, the B-1B would probably carry SRAM as well and fly direct from the United States. Cruising to hostile airspace at high altitude, the plane would probably refuel once from a tanker. Dropping low as it came within sight of enemy radar it might then fire SRAM missiles to attack the missile sites. Cleared to make an unchallenged penetration of enemy airspace, the bomber would fly a winding path to avoid known missile sites inland.

Approaching unseen, the B-1B would make a low run and drop its nuclear load on one or more targets. The B-1B can carry a truly astonishing warload. For instance, it can carry 38 nuclear bombs of such power that each would explode with 50 times the energy of the atom bombs dropped on Japan in 1945. One plane, therefore, can physically carry bombs totaling an explosive force nearly 2,000 times that of the bomb dropped on Hiroshima. A more usual load would involve a combination of SRAM and free-fall weapons, lowering the total number of bombs. Each bomb has a small parachute which slows it down, allowing the bomber to get away and escape the worst effects of the nuclear explosion.

Flying as evasive an escape path as it can, the B-1B would fly on to reach the airspace of a friendly country where it would then land. It would not have sufficient fuel to turn round and fly back out the way it came. Some SRAM missiles might be retained for helping it escape enemy airspace. Although crossing the border from inside rather than trying to penetrate from outside, enemy radar would still pick up the escaping bomber and attempt to shoot it down.

Although the B-52 would deploy stand-off weapons some distance away from enemy air space, they would nevertheless make use of hills and mountains to escape attacking fighters roaming far from home, endeavoring to prevent them releasing their weapons.

Future Bombers

Releasing free-fall gravity bombs, B-52 bombers may expose their crews to the blinding light of an atomic explosion and to prevent them having to look out the window special covers completely close the interior of the cockpit. To see where they are going, the crew would use special TV sets mounted on the display console showing the view seen from two special low-light cameras mounted in the nose section.

Some years ago it was believed the manned bomber no longer had a useful future. The advanced development of surface-to-air missiles seemed to threaten the bomber's existence, whatever it did to avoid detection. Then, further advances in electronics gave planes the means to jam radar, send confusing signals, or blind the scanners that continually search the sky. Called *countermeasures*, these activities provide a degree of protection by seeking to upset the early warning systems. Other ways of avoiding detection exist that are even more effective. A range of technologies called *Stealth* cover various ways of making a plane invisible to radar.

Radar detection works by reflecting radio signals off solid objects. As they bounce back they are picked up by antennas and appear on a radar screen like shapes or points of light. The form they take depends on the shape of the object from which they are reflected. For instance, an object with sharp corners or lines will stand out more than another object with rounded curves and no sharp points. Planes built like this are not easy to pick up on radar screens.

Conventional bombers, like the B-1B, are not specifically designed to have Stealth characteristics. They are, however, less visible than planes like the B-52. In fact, SAC's B-1B has only 1% the radar visibility of a B-52. This is both because it has more rounded curves and more important, because it has countermeasures which reduce its apparent size. To a radar operator, it would look like a large seabird. The only problem is that no known seabirds travel at Mach 1! What is really needed is something that is completely invisible to radar.

The United States is building such a bomber. It will probably look like a flying wing with no body. This the the best shape for low radar visibility. The engine inlets are probably on top of the plane, gracefully molded into the upper surface. Its surfaces will be well rounded, made of special materials that absorb radio waves to prevent them from bouncing back. The price for this invisibility will be paid in lower performance. The Stealth bomber probably has at most only one-third the bomb load of the B-1B and

The Soviet Union has begun large scale deployment of the Backfire bomber which could threaten the continental United States.

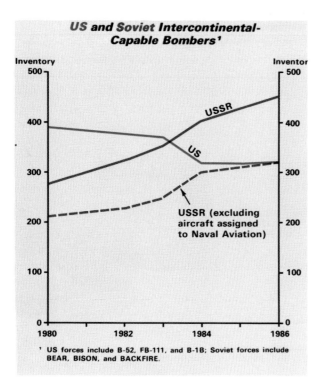

US and Soviet Intercontinental-Capable Bombers¹

Inventory

Inventor[y]

USSR

US

USSR (excluding aircraft assigned to Naval Aviation)

500
400
300
200
100
0

1980   1982   1984   1986

¹ US forces include B-52, FB-111, and B-1B; Soviet forces include BEAR, BISON, and BACKFIRE.

Emphasis in Soviet aviation on the long range bomber force has continued throughout the 1980s to the point where the respective strength of the two superpowers has been reversed, giving the Russians an advantage with their new high-performance planes.

much less range. However, survivability is more important than performance, and the Stealth bomber will get through more often than the B-1B. The air force will probably buy Stealth bombers by the end of this century.

The Russians are the only country other than the U.S. building big bombers. The Tupolev Backfire has been in service since 1975, and new planes have been added at the rate of 30 each year. By 1987, about 140 had been built. The Backfire has a top speed of Mach 1.9 and a range of 2,100 miles without refueling in the air. It will be joined by the much bigger Blackjack bomber. This plane is capable of Mach 2.1 and can strike targets 4,530 miles from base and return without refueling. If tankers are used, it has a much greater range.

The Russians operate a large number of older bombers. Called Bear and Bison, these planes have been around since 1955 and belong to the

same era as the B-52 in the United States. The Russians have about 700 medium and long-range bombers, while the United States has just over 300. Backfire and Blackjack will replace the older Soviet bombers, just as B-1B and Stealth will replace the B-52 in Strategic Air Command. These numbers are deceiving, however. The United States can station its bombers closer to Soviet territory than the Russians can to the United States. Some people believe this gives the United States an advantage, even though the Soviets have more than twice as many bombers.

The point to remember is that the Soviet Union is not the only country the United States might have to face, and that it needs long-range bombers to fly the very long distances that separate it from most other countries. The bomber force is important because it gives the air force an opportunity to control precisely the amount of force needed to deter aggression and use no more than necessary. That is a vital capability.

The latest Soviet bomber is called Blackjack, seen here in this artist's representation of preflight preparations at a Soviet air base.

The Blackjack is capable of attacking targets several thousand miles away from its base and in this artist's view is seen releasing a Soviet long range cruise missile.

ABBREVIATIONS

ALCM   Air Launched Cruise Missile

ICBM   Intercontinental Ballistic Missile

NASA   National Aeronautics Space Administration

NATO   North Atlantic Treaty Organization

SAC   Strategic Air Command

SAM   Surface-To-Air Missile

SLBM   Submarine Launched Ballistic Missile

SRAM   Short Range Attack Missile

GLOSSARY

ALCM	Air Launched Cruise Missiles dropped from a carrier-plane, at which point a small turbofan engine is used to propel the winged missile to its target more than 1,500 miles away. ALCM carries a nuclear warhead.
Area-rule	An aerodynamic design concept, in which the flow of air around the region where the wing joins the body of the plane is made smooth, enabling the plane to reach supersonic speed. Area-rule gives the plane a characteristic Coke-bottle shape.
Bogie	The assembly at the lower section of a main landing gear that contains all of the wheel and brake units.
Compression-lift	A method of gaining aerodynamic efficiency by designing a supersonic plane so that it rides on top of energy built up underneath its wing and body.
Countermeasures	In electronic warfare, any passive or active equipment designed to confuse or disturb radio signals broadcast from a transmitter with the object of detecting solid bodies. Basically, devices or equipment installed to help the carrier (such as a plane, ship, or tank) avoid detection.
Hydrogen bomb	A type of bomb in which energy is released by fusion of hydrogen nuclei to give helium nuclei. The energy required to start the fusion process is provided by an atom bomb that is surrounded by a hydrogen-containing substance such as lithium deuteride.
Lifting bodies	Aerodynamic research vehicles used by NASA and the air force and characterized by a blended wing-body generating lift over the total surface.
Mach	Mach 1, or unity, is the speed of sound: 760 MPH at sea level, decreasing to 660 MPH at a height of 36,000 feet. Mach 2.2 is equivalent to a speed of 1672 MPH at sea level or 1,452 MPH above 36,000 feet.
NATO	North Atlantic Treaty Organization formed in 1949 as an alliance of the U.S., Canada and West-European countries operating under a military pact whereby an attack on one is considered an attack on all.
SRAM	An abbreviation for Short Range Attack Missile, a rocket boosted projectile capable of flying more than 100 miles from release by a carrier-plane to its target.
Stand-off	In the context of a weapon, one that has its own propulsion which when released can transport a warhead to a target some distance away from the carrier-plane.
Stealth	A method of avoiding radar detection by blending wing, body, and external attachments into a smooth and rounded shape so that radio waves are not easily reflected back to a detector. Also refers to radio-absorbant materials which further reduce detection and special countermeasures equipment used to jam radar signals.
Turbofan	A jet engine with circular compressors to increase the volume of air taken in through the front, with burners behind the combustion chamber to give additional energy to the exhausted gases by reigniting them as they leave the nozzle.
Variable-geometry	A means by which the shape of an airplane wing can be changed in flight by attaching the wing to a pivot where it joins the main body (or fuselage) so it can be swivelled to any position. This wing design is also called the swing-wing.

INDEX

Page references in *italics* indicate photographs or illustrations.